big NATE

HUG IT OUT!

Complete Your *Big Nate* Collection

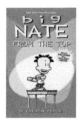  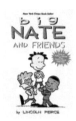   

 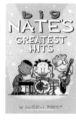 

big NATE
HUG IT OUT!

by LINCOLN PEIRCE

Andrews McMeel
PUBLISHING®

5

7

10

WHAT ARE YOU GUYS TALKING ABOUT?

OH, GIRL STUFF.

ELLEN'S WONDERING IF HER GORDIE IS "THE ONE."

YES. DEFINITELY YES.

GORDIE'S AWESOME. HE'S NICE, HE'S FUNNY, HE'S SMART. HE'S ELLEN'S PERFECT SOUL MATE.

HE ALSO GETS YOU FREE SWAG FROM THE COMICS STORE.

OKAY, SO HE'S **MY** PERFECT SOUL MATE. THE POINT IS, HE'S FAMILY.

Peirce

MR. AND MRS. WRIGHT, YOUR JOB ISN'T TO TALK TO THE KIDS ABOUT THE ART THEY'RE SEEING! THAT'S THE JOB OF THE MUSEUM DOCENTS!

YOUR ROLE IS SIMPLY TO KEEP TRACK OF YOUR GROUP, AND MAKE CERTAIN THE KIDS ARE WELL-BEHAVED AND RESPECTFUL!

WE CAN DO THAT!

MOD PAIN

AFTER ALL, WE RAISED TWO BOYS OF OUR OWN!

...ONE OF WHOM IS CURRENTLY BUTT-STUCK TO OUR SOFA PLAYING "WORLD OF WARCRAFT."

WE'RE TRYING TO BE PATIENT.

HI, BOYS AND GIRLS! I'M MRS. KELLEHER, AND I'M A DOCENT HERE AT THE MUSEUM!

I'LL BE SHOWING YOU SOME OF OUR WONDER-FUL PAINTINGS AND SCULPTURES, AND TELLING YOU ABOUT THE ARTISTS WHO CREATED THEM!

NOW BEFORE WE BEGIN, DOES ANYONE NEED TO USE THE RESTROOM?

YO.

WE'RE SENIORS. WE NEED OUR PIT STOPS.

IT'S AWFULLY NICE OF YOU AND YOUR WIFE TO CHAPERONE YOUR GRANDSON'S FIELD TRIP!

I LOVE IT WHEN THE MUSEUM HOSTS SCHOOL GROUPS! I USED TO BE A SCHOOLTEACHER MYSELF! THIRD AND FOURTH GRADE! THOSE CHILDREN WERE—

UM...

I'M SORRY, BUT THE BATTERY IN MY HEARING AID IS DEAD, SO I CAN'T UNDERSTAND A WORD YOU'RE SAYING.

YOU DON'T **HAVE** A HEARING AID, VERN.

SHE DOESN'T KNOW THAT.

HEY, LISTEN, BUDDY, I WASN'T TRYING TO CRITICIZE YOUR JOB A MINUTE AGO.

WHAT I **MEANT** WAS, IT'S A JOB THAT WOULD BE TOUGH FOR **ME. I** WOULDN'T LIKE IT!

BUT **YOU** LIKE IT, I CAN TELL! AND NO WONDER! IT'S A GOOD JOB! A **REAL** GOOD JOB!

MISTER, I JUST THREW UP BY THAT SCULPTURE OVER THERE.

WELL, GOTTA GO.

WHAT DO YOU THINK OF THE PAINTINGS, GRAMPS?

I LIKE THE OLD ONES. THE OLDER, THE BETTER.

IF A PAINTING'S, LIKE, A HUNDRED YEARS OLD OR MORE, I LIKE IT. BUT THE MODERN ONES, I DON'T GET.

I GENERALLY HAVE NO INTEREST IN STUFF THAT'S YOUNGER THAN I AM.

AND YET, HE FINDS A WAY TO ENJOY THE SPORTS ILLUSTRATED SWIMSUIT ISSUE.

I HAPPEN TO LIKE THE EXOTIC LOCATIONS.

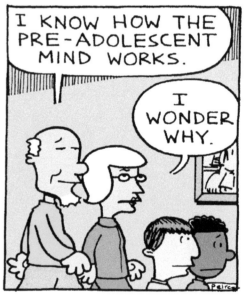

HEY, HERE COME LISA AND SALLY!

OOH! HOTTIE ALERT!

✶AHEM!✶ HI, LADIES.

HI, GUYS! WE'RE DOING A SPRING SPORTS PREVIEW FOR THE SCHOOL NEWSPAPER!

WILL YOU TELL OUR READERS YOUR GOALS FOR THE UPCOMING SEASON?

I WANT TO WIN EVERY GAME I PITCH AND BAT AT LEAST .350!

I WANT TO HIT OVER .400, DRIVE IN TWO RUNS PER GAME, AND WIN THE MVP AWARD!

WHAT ABOUT YOU, CHAD?

ME?

I JUST WANT TO HAVE FUN AND HELP MY TEAM ANY WAY I CAN!

AWW!

THAT'S SO SWEET!

CAN I CHANGE MY ANSWER?

CHAD'S CHADNESS IS HARD TO COMPETE WITH.

37

Chapter 1

Private Charles "Chuck" Manley's chest swelled with pride as he pulled on his blue woolen uniform after washing his face in the slow-moving waters of Bull Run Creek.

"I can't believe I am actually a member of the Union Army and that we are about to do battle against the gray-clad soldiers of the Confederacy!" he thought to himself while enjoying a hearty breakfast.

A gun roared in the distance, and suddenly a cannonball flew by, knocking his donut from his hand. It landed on the ground and got all covered with dirt and mud, making it all gross and stuff.

It was going to be a long war.

Private Charles "Chuck" Manley couldn't understand what was happening that fateful day at Gettysburg. Again and again he had fired his rifle, but he kept missing his target.

Then, inside his head, he heard the voice of General Ulysses S. Grant. "Trust the Force, Chuck," it told him. "Trust the Force." Chuck closed his eyes and squeezed the trigger.

When he opened his eyes again, he found that he'd shot one of his own men by mistake. Luckily, it was only a flesh wound. Anyway, about five minutes later, the Rebels retreated.

Chuck smiled knowingly. Yes, the Force was indeed strong in Gettysburg that day.

MR. GALVIN, ARE WE **REALLY** HAVING A QUIZ TODAY?

YES, INDEED. YOU'VE KNOWN ABOUT IT FOR OVER A WEEK.

BUT WE DIDN'T FINISH THE IN-CLASS REVIEW!

YEAH!

YOU SHOULD HAVE FINISHED THE REVIEW ON YOUR OWN.

PLUS, YOU NEVER EXPLAINED PART 2 OF CHAPTER 12 BECAUSE OF THAT FIRE DRILL, REMEMBER?

EVERYTHING YOU NEED TO KNOW ABOUT CHAPTER 12 IS IN THE TEXTBOOK.

BUT THE TEXTBOOK IS SO **CONFUSING**!

NOT IF YOU READ IT CAREFULLY. SIT DOWN, BOYS.

HE'S GOING THROUGH WITH THE QUIZ.

WE'RE DEAD.

LEAVE THIS TO ME, BOYS!

MR. GALVIN, WILL YOU TELL US ABOUT THE TIME YOU SHARED A CAB WITH FLORENCE HENDERSON?

IT WAS A WINDSWEPT DAY ON THE SIDEWALKS OF MANHATTAN...

YOU'RE A GENIUS.

SO TRUE.

NATE, I'M SORRY YOU SLIPPED ON A WET FLOOR, BUT THAT HARDLY ENTITLES YOU TO **SUE** THE **SCHOOL**!

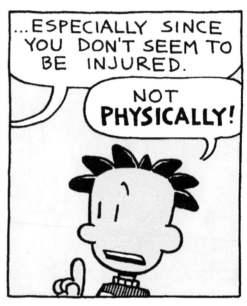

...ESPECIALLY SINCE YOU DON'T SEEM TO BE INJURED.

NOT **PHYSICALLY**!

...BUT WHAT ABOUT MY **EMOTIONAL** TRAUMA?

EMOTIONAL TRAUMA?

FROM A PUDDLE?

NO, NO, FROM MRS. GODFREY. I SWITCHED ISSUES.

I WANT TO SUE THE SCHOOL, AND **YOU** DON'T WANT ME TO! MAYBE WE CAN COMPROMISE!

IF YOU WERE TO... ✕ AHEM! ✕ ... GIVE ME A **SETTLEMENT**, YOU WOULDN'T HAVE TO GO THROUGH A MESSY **TRIAL**!

UH-HUH. WHAT'D YOU HAVE IN MIND?

A MODEST CASH PAYMENT OF 25,000 DOLLARS.

HOW 'BOUT YOU JUST LEAVE MY OFFICE BEFORE I THROW YOUR BUTT IN DETENTION?

THAT WORKS TOO.

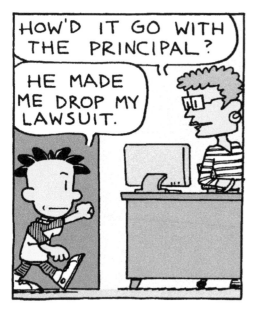

HOW'D IT GO WITH THE PRINCIPAL?

HE MADE ME DROP MY LAWSUIT.

IT'S NOT **FAIR**! IT'S THE **SCHOOL'S** FAULT THAT I SLIPPED AND FELL! I SHOULD BE **PAID** FOR MY PAIN AND SUFFERING!

IT WOULDN'T HAVE TO BE A **BIG** PAYMENT! IT WOULDN'T EVEN HAVE TO BE **MONEY**! IT COULD BE JUST A SMALL...UH... TOKEN OF... Y'KNOW...

I HAVE HALF A ROLL OF MENTOS IN MY PURSE.

DEAL!

Peirce

...AND RIGHT HERE, ALMOST INVISIBLE TO THE NAKED EYE, WAS A **PUDDLE**! MY FOOT HIT IT, AND **DOWN I WENT**!

OH. HI.

I WONDER IF PRIVATE SCHOOL PRINCIPALS HAVE THESE PROBLEMS.

MY HEAD HIT THE FLOOR, AND EVERYTHING WENT DARK...

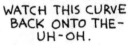

HERE'S AN INTERESTING FACT ABOUT CALVIN COOLIDGE!...

FRANCIS, **STOP!** WE DON'T NEED TO HEAR ANY OF YOUR USELESS TRIVIA!

THE ONLY GOOD TRIVIA IS TRIVIA ABOUT "STAR TREK: THE NEXT GENERATION."

WHAT?

WHAT MAKES COUNSELOR DEANNA TROI **GOOD** TRIVIA AND CALVIN COOLIDGE **BAD** TRIVIA?

CALVIN COOLIDGE DIDN'T DO HIS JOB IN A SKIN-TIGHT UNITARD.

CLEAVAGE ONE, COOLIDGE ZERO!

IT'S **RIDICULOUS** THAT YOU ONLY PAY ATTENTION TO "STAR TREK: THE NEXT GENERATION" TRIVIA!

THAT'S THE WAY I AM, FRANCIS.

BUT THERE'S **SO MUCH** GOOD TRIVIA OUT THERE! LET ME **SHARE** IT WITH YOU!

NO! I'M NOT LISTENING!

JUST LET ME TELL YOU ONE THING! ONE FACTOID!

NO! CUT IT OUT!

CALVIN COOLIDGE IS THE ONLY PRESIDENT BORN ON THE 4TH OF JULY!

HELP!

NOW DO YOU ADMIT A LITTLE TRIVIA CAN COME IN **HANDY** SOMETIMES?

THANKS TO MY CALVIN COOLIDGE TRIVIA, YOU JUST GOT EXTRA CREDIT FROM MRS. GODFREY!

OKAY, OKAY! YOU'RE **RIGHT!**

BUT THAT DOESN'T MEAN I WANT YOU **BURYING** ME WITH PILES OF USELESS FACTS ABOUT CALVIN COOLIDGE!

...WHO, BY THE WAY, HAD A PET **RACCOON** NAMED REBECCA WHO USED TO WANDER AROUND THE WHITE HOUSE! NOT ONLY THAT...

STOP. STOP. STOP.

63

WHAT'S OUR PLAN B?

WHATTA YA MEAN?

THIS IS PRIVATE PROPERTY! WHERE ARE WE GONNA PLAY FRISBEE GOLF IF THIS GUY KICKS US OFF HIS LAND?

TEDDY! RE**LAX**!

THIS GUY'S A **HIPPIE**! HE'S, LIKE, ALL GRANOLA AND WHATNOT! HE'S AN **ORGANIC FARMER**!

SO?

SO, HIPPIES AND FRISBEES GO TOGETHER!

ZING!

THIS GUY WON'T MIND A FEW FRISBEES FLYING AROUND! HE'LL PROBABLY WANT TO **JOIN** US!

ZWING!

TRUST ME, THIS GUY WON'T KICK US OFF HIS LAND! WE WON'T **NEED** A PLAN B!

HOW ABOUT A PLAN C?

I THOUGHT HIPPIES WERE SUPPOSED TO BE MELLOW.

CHEEZ DOODLES HAVE GOT TO BE THE LEAST DIGNIFIED SNACK OF ALL TIME.

THEY LEAVE ORANGE POWDER ALL OVER EVERYTHING. THEY STAIN YOUR CLOTHES. THEY STAIN YOUR SKIN.

MUNCH MUNCH MUNCH MUNCH MUNCH

THEY GET STUCK IN YOUR TEETH AND STAY THERE FOR HOURS! THEY MAKE YOUR BREATH SMELL LIKE TUBE SOCKS! FRANKLY, THEY'RE DISGUSTING!

OH, HOW I LOVE THEM.

HE MAKES THIS SPEECH EVERY DAY.

HOW CAN YOU BE SICK OF CHEEZ DOODLES? YOU EAT 'EM **EVERY DAY!**

MAYBE THAT'S THE PROBLEM, TEDDY.

HE'S EATEN SO **MANY** OF THEM, THEY'VE COMPLETELY LOST THEIR APPEAL!

I CAN'T ACCEPT THAT.

PEOPLE DON'T GO FROM **LOVING** SOMETHING TO **HATING** IT IN **FIVE SECONDS!**

P...PETE CARROLL.

YEAH! PETE CARROLL!

WE'RE NOT TALKING ABOUT THAT!!

FOR MY ENTIRE LIFE, WHENEVER I LOOKED AT A CHEEZ DOODLE, I FELT **HAPPY!**

NOW, I'M **SICKENED!** I'M **NAUSEATED!** I'M **REPULSED!**

SNIFF! SNIFF!

I'M INTRIGUED!

HE'S BACK.

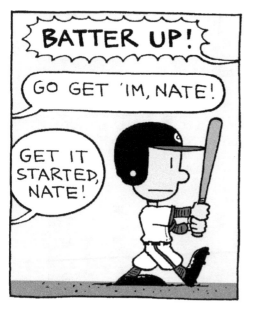

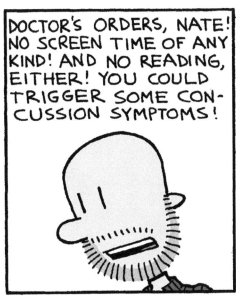

LISTEN TO THIS, TEDDY! HEH HEH HEH HEH HEH.

WHAT **IS** THAT?

THAT, MY FRIEND, IS A **WARM CHUCKLE!**

UH... OKAY.

I'VE BEEN WORKING ON IT FOR **WEEKS!** I'VE ALWAYS WANTED TO HAVE A WARM CHUCKLE IN MY BAG OF TRICKS!

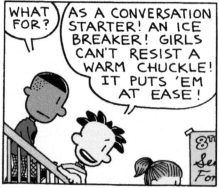

WHAT FOR?

AS A CONVERSATION STARTER! AN ICE BREAKER! GIRLS CAN'T RESIST A WARM CHUCKLE! IT PUTS 'EM AT EASE!

WATCH HOW IT WORKS ON THOSE LOVELY LADIES OVER THERE!

I BARELY **NOTICED** IT!

WELL, **I** NOTICE IT!

HEH HEH HEH HEH HEH

!

HANDY TIP: DON'T USE YOUR WARM CHUCKLE ON A GIRL WHO'S UPSET ABOUT A REALLY BIG ZIT ON HER FOREHEAD.

TRASH

I'M SURE YOU'RE AWARE, NATE, THAT YOU'RE IN DANGER OF NEEDING TO ATTEND SUMMER SCHOOL.

UH HUH.

I'D SAY SOME TUTORING IS IN ORDER BEFORE THE FINAL EXAM.

OKAY, I'LL ASK FRANCIS.

NO. YOU AND FRANCIS ARE FRIENDS. YOU'LL ONLY END UP **DISTRACTING** EACH OTHER.

I'LL SELECT YOUR TUTOR.

NO. NO. NO. NO. NO. NO.

RRRRINNNG!

THERE'S THE BELL. THAT'S ENOUGH FOR NOW.

FOR **NOW**? THAT'S ENOUGH, **PERIOD!**

TWENTY MINUTES OF TUTORING DURING **LUNCH** DOESN'T GET YOU READY FOR THE FINAL EXAM, PINHEAD! IT TAKES **HOURS** OF WORK **OUTSIDE** OF SCHOOL!

I'LL BE AT YOUR HOUSE AT 4:00 THIS AFTERNOON.

OOOOOH!

I CAN'T TAKE IT.

SUMMER SCHOOL?

YEAH, BUT MRS. GODFREY SAID I CAN AVOID IT!

WELL, I WOULD **HOPE** SO!

I NEED TO GET AN A ON THE FINAL.

GINA'S COMING OVER TO TUTOR ME.

GOOD, GOOD. LET'S GET READY.

WE'LL MOVE ALL THIS STUFF TO GIVE YOU PLENTY OF SPACE!

OKAY, SPREAD OUT ALL YOUR CLASS NOTES ON THE TABLE.

I THINK I SEE THE PROBLEM.

IN MY DEFENSE, THAT'S ONLY MY SECOND SEMESTER NOTES. I LOST MY STUFF FROM THE FIRST SEMESTER.

OKAY, LET'S TALK ABOUT THE BOSTON MASSACRE.

AH.

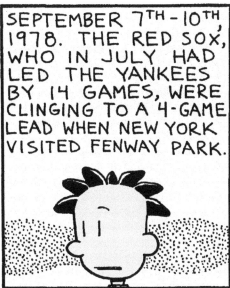

SEPTEMBER 7TH-10TH, 1978. THE RED SOX, WHO IN JULY HAD LED THE YANKEES BY 14 GAMES, WERE CLINGING TO A 4-GAME LEAD WHEN NEW YORK VISITED FENWAY PARK.

THE YANKEES SWEPT THE 4-GAME SERIES, SCORING A TOTAL OF 42 RUNS. BOSTON SCORED ONLY 9 RUNS AND COMMITTED 12 ERRORS. IT WAS A NIGHTMARE.

CRIPES.

MY DAD'S **STILL** NOT OVER IT.

WELL, YOU'RE AS READY AS YOU'LL EVER BE.

I'VE DONE ALL I CAN.

ALL **YOU** CAN?

YOU TOLD ME WHICH NAMES AND DATES TO MEMORIZE! THAT'S **IT**! I DID ALL THE **WORK**!

WHEN I ACE THE SOCIAL STUDIES FINAL, IT WON'T BE BECAUSE OF YOUR SO-CALLED **TUTORING**!

IT'LL BE BECAUSE OF **ONE THING**:

MY SUPERIOR BRAINPOWER!

RATTLE

RATTLE! RATTLE!

DING DONG

HAPPY LAST
DAY OF SCHOOL

TOO BAD WE DIDN'T HAVE TIME FOR ANY PRANKS THIS YEAR.

I SNUCK IN A FEW.

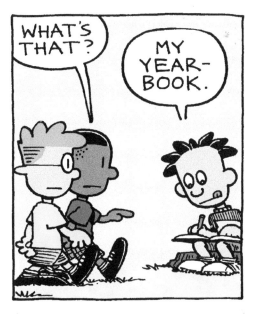

OOH! CAN I SIGN YOUR YEARBOOK, NATE?

SORRY, CHAD, I ALREADY DID IT FOR YOU.

WHAT?

IT WAS A TIMESAVER TO WRITE EVERYONE'S INSCRIPTION MYSELF. SEE?

DEAR NATE— YOU ARE THE RAINBOW JIMMIES ON THE CUPCAKE OF LIFE.
— CHAD

THAT **DOES** SOUND LIKE ME!

I AIM TO PLEASE!

113

KNOCK DOWN THE PINS! WIN A PRIZE!

I'LL TRY IT!

CLUNK!

YES!

CLUNK!

YES!

CLONK!!

YES!

CONGRATULATIONS, CHAMP. THAT WINS YOU ONE TOKEN.

A TOKEN?

BUT I WANT THAT SKATEBOARD UP THERE!

THE SKATEBOARD? THEN YOU'VE GOT SOME **WORK** TO DO, SONNY!

THAT'S A TWENTY TOKEN PRIZE! YOU'RE NINETEEN SHORT!

WHAT?

WELL, WHAT KIND OF PRIZE CAN I GET FOR **ONE** TOKEN?

TWO MINUTES LATER...

IT WAS EITHER THIS OR A PAIR OF WAX LIPS.

WHERE'D SHE GO? SHE WAS **RIGHT HERE!**

WHO?

THE GIRL I WAS ON THE **RIDE** WITH! SHE **DISAPPEARED!**

SO? NO WORRIES, JUST LOOK HER UP ON THE INTERNET!

YOU GOT HER NAME, RIGHT?

WHAP!

ARE YOU SURE THIS ISN'T LIKE THAT TIME YOU HAD AN IMAGINARY FRIEND?

SCHOOL PICTURE GUY!

AH! WHAT'S HAPPENING, AMIGO?

FSSSss

DOING YOUR BALLOON SCULPTURES AGAIN THIS YEAR, HUH?

YES INDEED!

Loon BALL

AND LET ME TELL YOU, KID, I'M IN **HEAVEN!** THIS SURE BEATS TAKING PICTURES!

SCHOOL PICTURE DAY IS A NIGHTMARE OF CRUSTY NOSES AND SWEATY FOREHEADS! THE KIDS **HATE** IT! HALF OF 'EM END UP IN **TEARS!**

BUT HERE AT THE FAIR, THERE ARE NO TEARS IN SIGHT! **ALL** THE KIDS LOVE LOONEY, THE BALLOON SCULPTOR!

MISTER, CAN YOU MAKE ME A BALLOON HAT?

ABSOLUTELY, M'BOY! I'LL CREATE A CROWN FIT FOR A **KING!**

SKWEE SKWOK SKWEE

WEAR IT WITH PRIDE!

POP!

APPARENTLY, MY LIMITED EDITION "GREEN LANTERN" RING HAS A SHARP EDGE I HADN'T ACCOUNTED FOR.

I CAN'T GIVE UP ON THE GIRL I MET AT THE FAIR! WHAT IF SHE'S MY **SOUL MATE?**

WHAT IF IT'S **DESTINY** FOR HER AND ME TO END UP TOGETHER? I'VE GOT TO **DO** SOMETHING!

NO, YOU DON'T. IF IT'S DESTINY, THAT MEANS IT'LL HAPPEN REGARDLESS OF WHAT YOU DO.

BUT THAT'S NO FUN.

IF YOU REALLY WANT TO DO SOMETHING, YOU CAN GET ME A SNICKERS BAR FROM THE SNACK SHACK!

I'M GOING BACK TO THE FAIRGROUNDS. A GOOD PRIVATE EYE LEAVES NO STONE UNTURNED!

I'LL THOROUGHLY INTERVIEW EVERY SINGLE EMPLOYEE! SOMEONE MUST HAVE SEEN SOMETHING!

THE FAIR LEFT TOWN THREE DAYS AGO, KID.

IT'S LIKE WATCHING A BLOODHOUND WITH NO SENSE OF SMELL.

LOOK AROUND, BOYS. MAYBE SHE DROPPED HER WALLET.

HERE'S A WEBSITE FOR PEOPLE WITH MISSED CONNECTIONS.

"MISSED CONNECTIONS"?

YEAH— LIKE **MY** SITUATION! YOU MEET SOMEONE BRIEFLY BUT DON'T QUITE MAKE A CONNECTION! THIS WEBSITE HELPS PEOPLE WITH THAT!

LIKE **THIS** GUY: "YOU WERE A STUNNING THIRTYISH REDHEAD. I WAS A MID-THIRTIES HIPPIE WITH A DENIM VEST. OUR EYES MET DURING A CROWDED SUBWAY RIDE...

...ON JUNE 12TH, 1973."

IS IT JUST ME, OR DOES IT SMELL DESPERATE IN HERE?

CARE TO BUY A NEWSPAPER, MR. EUSTIS?

A NEWSPAPER?

YUP! EVERYBODY SAYS NEWSPAPERS ARE DYING, BUT I'M HERE TO SAY THEY'RE GOIN' STRONG!

"THE NATELY NEWS"!

MY OWN PUBLICATION! I'M THE FOUNDER!

I'M ALSO THE EDITOR-IN-CHIEF, THE NEWS REPORTER, THE SPORTS COLUMNIST, THE STAFF PHOTOGRAPHER, AND THE CARTOONIST!

BUT IT'S EXPENSIVE TO RUN A NEWSPAPER. ISN'T THAT WHY SO MANY OF THEM ARE STRUGGLING?

I WON'T HAVE THAT PROBLEM!

MY ONLY EXPENSE IS MY OWN SALARY! SO IT'LL BE EASY FOR ME TO MAKE A PROFIT!

OKAY, I'LL TAKE ONE. HOW MUCH?

FORTY-THREE DOLLARS.

I THINK I SEE A FLAW IN YOUR BUSINESS PLAN.

CAN I INTEREST YOU IN A DAILY SUBSCRIPTION?

SORRY, KID, IF I LET YOU SING ON THE AIR, THE STATION MANAGER WILL SHOW ME THE DOOR.

YEAH, THAT'S WHAT SIR ROCKS-A-LOT SAID.

HERE'S WHAT I **CAN** DO, THOUGH: I WILL TELL YOUR STORY AND DEDICATE A SONG TO YOUR ELUSIVE MYSTERY GIRL!

YOU **WILL?**

ABSOTIVELY, MY FRIEND! NOW SIT BACK AND WATCH THE MAGIC HAPPEN!

WOW!

FIRST, THOUGH, I GOTTA READ AN EX-LAX SPOT.

ON THE AIR

... AND WHEN MY LOVE-STRUCK FRIEND TURNED AROUND, THE FETCHING YOUNG LADY WHO'D BEEN ALONGSIDE HIM IN THE "FLAMETHROWER" WAS **GONE!**

HE DESCRIBES HER AS ABOUT FOUR AND A HALF FEET TALL, WITH HAIR PULLED BACK IN A PONYTAIL AND A BUTTON NOSE!

AS FOR MY CHUM HERE, HE'S ROUGHLY THE SAME HEIGHT, A BIT SCRAWNY, WITH HAIR RESEMBLING A TANGLED MASS OF JET-BLACK SEAWEED!

WHA-?

HEY!

IT'S RADIO, M'BOY. THEATER OF THE MIND.

145

STILL HAVEN'T FOUND YOUR MYSTERY GIRL, HUH?

NO. I'M STARTING TO LOSE HOPE.

I MEAN, IT'S ALREADY BEEN A **MONTH** SINCE I MET HER AT THE FAIR!

WOULD YOU EVEN **RECOGNIZE** HER AT THIS POINT?

OH, I'D RECOGNIZE HER, ALL RIGHT. ONCE I SEE A FACE, I NEV—

HEY, WHO'S THAT?

YOUR GRANDMA MUST HAVE BEEN HAPPY WHEN SHE SAW HOW THIN YOU GOT AT LAKE BEEWELL, CHAD.

BUT **I'M** NOT HAPPY!

I LIKED MYSELF THE WAY I **WAS!** I GOT PLENTY OF EXERCISE!... I ATE LOTS OF HEALTHY FOODS!...

...BUT I DIDN'T COUNT EVERY CALORIE IN A **FOOD JOURNAL!** AND IF I WANTED AN OREO, I **ATE** AN OREO!

IS THAT SO WRONG?

WHAT'D YOUR GRAND-MOTHER SAY WHEN SHE SAW YOU'D REGAINED THE WEIGHT YOU LOST?

SHE WASN'T HAPPY!

SHE SAID IT SHOWS THAT I'M WEAK. SHE TOLD ME I HAVE NO WILLPOWER.

THEN I REMINDED HER THAT HER NEW YEAR'S RESOLUTION TO GIVE UP CHEWING TOBACCO LASTED THREE HOURS.

WELL PLAYED, CHAD!

IT WAS THE BEST TALK WE'VE EVER HAD!

I CAN'T BELIEVE SCHOOL STARTS TOMORROW.

I WISH I KNEW IN ADVANCE WHAT IT'S GONNA BE LIKE THIS YEAR.

HEY! SPITSY! MAYBE **YOU** CAN HELP ME! ANIMALS SUPPOSEDLY CAN **SENSE** STUFF LIKE THIS!

WURF!

WHAT DO YOUR INSTINCTS TELL YOU? AM I GONNA HAVE A GOOD YEAR OR A BAD YEAR?

ON A SCALE OF ONE TO TEN! BARK ONCE FOR AN AWFUL YEAR, TEN TIMES FOR A GREAT YEAR!

SNIFFA SNUFFA

OWOOOOO

I CAN'T TAKE IT.

I'M GETTING A PREMONITION ABOUT THAT GIRL I MET AT THE FAIR!

OH, YEAH?

YUP! I'VE GOT A FEELING SHE'S GOING TO END UP RIGHT HERE AT P.S. 38!

AS A NEW STUDENT, YOU MEAN?

RIGHT! SHE PROBABLY MOVED TO TOWN OVER THE SUMMER!

I'LL BET WHEN I TURN AROUND, SHE'LL BE **RIGHT THERE**!

WELL, HELLO, NATE! WELCOME BACK!

MRS. SHIPULSKI, ARE THERE ANY NEW KIDS IN SIXTH GRADE THIS YEAR?

WHY, **YES**, AS A MATTER OF FACT! THERE **IS** A NEW STUDENT!

THERE **IS**?

AND HERE HE IS! NATE, THIS IS JUSTIN! HE'S JUST MOVED HERE FROM OHIO!

I'M SURE THE TWO OF YOU WILL GET ALONG **VERY**—

NO, THIS WON'T WORK. GOT ANY OTHERS?

SHOVE!

Peirce

...AND WHEN I RODE THE FLAMETHROWER, I ENDED UP SITTING NEXT TO THIS GIRL! I DIDN'T KNOW HER, BUT SHE WAS CUTE! **WICKED** CUTE!

AND WE GOT ALONG **GREAT!** I MEAN, THE RIDE ONLY LASTED A COUPLE MINUTES, BUT THERE WAS **CHEMISTRY** BETWEEN US! I COULD **FEEL** IT!

THEN THE RIDE ENDED, AND I LOST HER IN THE CROWD! SHE DISAPPEARED BEFORE I COULD EVEN FIND OUT HER **NAME!**

SO I SAID TO MY- SELF: I'M GOING TO TRACK HER DOWN IF IT'S THE LAST THING

ALL I ASKED WAS "HOW WAS YOUR SUMMER?"

YAK YAK YAK YAK YAK YAK YAK AK YAK YAK YAK YAK

YOU'RE LUCKY, SHERMAN.

YOU DON'T HAVE TO EXPERIENCE HOW IT FEELS TO THINK YOU MIGHT REALLY LIKE SOMEONE...

...ONLY TO **LOSE** HER BEFORE YOU EVEN GET TO **KNOW** HER!

RIGHT. WHAT WOULD A GERBIL KNOW ABOUT BEING SEPARATED FROM HIS PEERS?

IS IT JUST ME, OR IS HE MAKING A SARCASTIC FACE?

PRINCIPAL NICHOLS, EDUCATION IS SUPPOSED TO BE FUN, RIGHT?

IT CERTAINLY **CAN** BE!

SO IF I'M NOT HAVING FUN IN A CLASS, THAT MEANS THE TEACHER'S DOING A LOUSY JOB, RIGHT?

UH... WELL, I—

AND IF A TEACHER'S DOING A LOUSY JOB, SHE SHOULD BE **FIRED**, RIGHT?

"SHE"?

OR HE. IF YOU WANT TO TURF MR. GALVIN, TOO, I'M GOOD WITH THAT.

AREN'T YOU **HOT**, PRINCIPAL NICHOLS?

IT'S, LIKE, NINETY DEGREES AND YOU'RE WEARING A **JACKET**!

I SUPPOSE IT **IS** A BIT STUFFY IN THE HALLWAY...

...BUT I'M ON MY WAY TO MY OFFICE, WHICH IS AIR-CONDITION—

WHAT?

OOPSY.

NATE, DID I SEE YOU AND GINA ARGUING JUST NOW?

UH... YEAH, BUT—

NO **BUTS,** YOUNG MAN! THERE ARE NO EXCUSES FOR **INSULTING** SOMEONE!

YOU MAY NOT CALL GINA NAMES, CRITICIZE HER, OR DEMEAN HER IN ANY WAY!

WELL, WHAT **CAN** I DO?

I DON'T HAVE A LIST, IF THAT'S WHAT YOU MEAN.

CAN I TELL HER THERE'S FOOD ON HER FACE WHEN THERE REALLY ISN'T?

COACH CALHOUN'S IN A MEETING, TROOPS. **I'LL** RUN PRACTICE TODAY!

I KNOW, I KNOW! YOU THINK I'M TOO **STRICT**! YOU DON'T LIKE MY "OLD SCHOOL" APPROACH!

WELL, I'M NO **FOOL**, GENTS! I CAN SEE THAT TIMES ARE CHANGING! COACHING IS **DIFFERENT** NOW!

YOU'RE NOT SUPPOSED TO **YELL** AT KIDS ANYMORE! COACHES HAVE TO LEARN TO **COMMUNICATE!**

AND WE CAN'T OVER-EMPHASIZE **WINNING** THE WAY WE USED TO! THE POINT IS FOR YOU TO HAVE **FUN!**

SO **BELIEVE** ME, I GET IT! I KNOW ABOUT ALL THESE NEW TRENDS IN COACHING!...

...AND I REJECT THEM COMPLETELY. LINE UP FOR WIND SPRINTS.

RUN!

I NO LONGER PITY THE KIDS ON THE CROSS COUNTRY TEAM.

Andrews McMeel Publishing
a division of Andrews McMeel Universal
1130 Walnut Street, Kansas City, Missouri 64106

www.andrewsmcmeel.com

ISBN: 978-1-5248-5578-9

Library of Congress Control Number: 2019934074

These strips appeared in newspapers from
March 15, 2015, through September 13, 2015.

Big Nate can be viewed on the Internet at
www.gocomics.com/big_nate.

Check out these and other books from Andrews McMeel Publishing

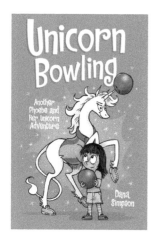

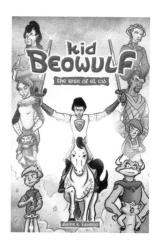